Frankly Speaking: Learning To Fly Again (Volume One)

Harper Starlight

I WANT TO THANK MY PARENTS, MY FAMILY AND
FRIENDS FOR THEIR LOVE, CARE, SUPPORT, GUIDANCE
AND INSPIRATION…YOU ALL TRULY ARE MY ANGELS IN
THE WINGS.

CONTENTS

1.It's not as though I never loved you.

It's not as though I never loved you,
With your death, my love dissolved over time...
It was never my intention to lose you, it just
happens as time passes by...
I learnt to bury you, effortlessly.
As my tears escape me, as this grief diminishes,
As my love for you withers,
It surpasses me,
With your death.
This mourning pierces your memories until there is
no more...
It all fades into the present.
The grief demolishes the insides till there's nothing
left,
It may seem like I never loved you,
As my love perishes in time,
My tears draw to a close.
The guilt deepens inside till there's nothing left...
But, your death passing me by...
Then I'll confess it was never my intention to lose
you.
It's not as though I never loved you...
I've just surrendered to time.

2.Goodbye Part One.

It's been a while, I've been lacking the words and
courage to say goodbye.
It's been a while since I heard the pain dissemble
your voice.
But your voice never shook with fear and sorrow.
Still I've been lacking the words and the courage to
say goodbye.

We always believed we would overcome all of life's
challenges.
How wrong were we?
How wrong were we?

My dear Theresa,
You were always caring, considerate, thoughtful and
understanding.
I do remember our time together and as always you
gave me words of strength.
I'm thankful for our conversations
I hope and pray that dear God and the universe
take care of your precious and beloved soul.
Still it feels like I've been lacking the words and the
courage to say goodbye.

My dear Theresa,
I'm praying for your soul and spirit,
And always you're giving me words of
encouragement, wisdom and intelligence to

continue to lead my life.
I only hope I have reciprocated it.
I'm thankful for our conversations, as kind and
fond memories are all I have left.
I hope and pray that dear God and the universe
takes care of your precious and beloved soul.
Still it feels like I've been lacking the words and the
courage to say goodbye.

It feels like dear God and the universe never gave
us enough time to evolve together.
I've just realised how much I missed you.
There is a gaping hole in my life.
I'm missing you shrewdness, your intellect and your
calmness.
I'm thankful for all our conversations together.
It feels like dear God and the universe never gave
us enough time to evolve together.
Still it feels like I've been lacking the words and the
courage to say goodbye.

Now I must carry on alone fighting and combating
my inner demons.
I will always remember that dear God and the
beautiful universe presented me with one of the
greatest gifts of all...
Your life, your existence,
And this I shall cherish and treasure for the
reminder of my days

Yet it still feels like I've been lacking the words and the courage to say goodbye.

<u>3.Why I walked away.</u>

You need to hear, know and respect my reasons
and decisions.
You are no longer in control of me and my destiny
I am!
With your bruises and scars you left memorable
imprints on my body.
You signified I was yours to manhandle and to have
power over.
It wasn't just physically that I felt weighed down by
a tonne.
Verbally you are equally as scarring in my mind and
underneath the skin
All the many ways you disrespected me hidden
within.

You ruled me with the hand of fear and fist of fire.
I was constantly and consistently afraid
And terrified of doing something that would trigger
your temper or anger.
This happened frequently.
I found myself shaking with panic.
I found my confidence and faith in humanity
shrinking and diminishing physically and mentally.
My love for you transgressed into hate, disgust and
revulsion.
I lost all respect I had for you.
I grew tired of hiding your bruises
As it dawned on me I realised this is no way for

anyone to live
No one should oppress, dominate and hold sway
over any human being.
These are the reasons why I've decided to leave you

With your bruises and scars you left unforgettable
wounds and blemishes on my body.
You signified I was yours to manipulate and reign
over.
It wasn't just physically that I felt weighed down by
a load
Verbally you are equally as mutilating in my mind
and underneath the skin
All the many ways you disrespected me hidden
within.

Now you are begging and pleading for me to stay.
It's too late all the love I had has disappeared and
vanished
In this frozen heart.
It no longer matters how much you tell me that you
love me and cannot live without me.
You need to hear, know and respect my reasons
and decisions.
You are no longer in control of me and my destiny
I am!
And I'm leaving you!

4.Rebuild.

The sight of dust is all that remains.
It seems like everything I worked for went up in
smoke in this crippled mind.
Maybe now there's a different lesson for me to
learn.
It's time to get up now.
Rebuild, Rebuild
I can't give up now.
Except I've lost my compass,
I have no sense of direction.
Show me where to go?
Tell me what to believe?
I need to believe
I can't give up now
I've got to rebuild.
I feel the burning of the sunlight against my soul,
I fear the terror in the rain,
I am my own wrath,
I am my own fury.
I'm waning,
I'm in pieces.
And there's no one but myself to blame.
As I watch the doubt unsettle me,
As it engages me,
I'll remember I'm not the first and I will not be the
last.
I can't give up now,
It's time to be courageous.

It's time to rebuild.
I know life is a journey for which there is no map.
No one can tell you how to live especially once
you've snapped.
Sometimes you have to go back to the beginning,
To see what you never noticed before,
To loose it all to understand,
That the greatest lesson is to know how to live.
It's time to gather up all the courage and summon
all the faith you have.
Don't give up now.
Rebuild.

5.Cherish

We were a group of people bounded together by conditions
Through the deep rooted pain and agony
And here we found sarcasm, derision and laughter
Regardless of our problems.
We didn't always need to discuss this as we put it to lay down on the side.
It's here we found a deeper and meaningful friendship.
The kind that you can even appreciate and cherish today.
Because when we needed laughter and delight you were there
And when we needed to open up about the anguish you were there.
Very few people would understand where we've been
Very few people make an effort to...
Unfortunately the truth is you can't until you've been there...

We were a group of people bounded by the circumstances
Through the deep rooted anguish and heartache
And here we found irony, mockery and amusement
Regardless of our problems.
We didn't always need to discuss this as we put it to lay down on the side.

It's here we found profound companionship.
The kind that you can even treasure and cherish today.
Because when we needed distraction and pleasure you were there
And when we needed to open up about the sorrow you were there.
Very few people would understand where we've been
Very few people make an effort to...
Unfortunately the truth is you can't until you've been there...

6.Another Continent.

I wish I had told you that I cherished and prized all
the many ways you cared for me,
Prior to you leaving.
I wish I had expressed my gratitude to you for the
support and sustenance you gave to me.
Now you are a world away from me…
On another continent.

I long to tell you how much I admired, revered and
respected you,
Before you departed on your journey.
I have no idea if you received my note before you
left.
I wish I had spoken to you and recognised you for
all you have done for me.
Now you are a world away from me…
On another continent.

I know I'm not the only one you maintained and
sustained,
And that you always tried to light up our
pathways…
Even if life felt like it was all over and there was no
more left to give …
I want you to know how treasured you are and how
grateful and indebted we are.
Now you are a world away from me…
On another continent.

I yearn to tell you that I'm not in love with you,
But I adore you and I hold you in great esteem and
regard.
Now this no longer matters.
Now you are a world away from me…
On another continent.

7.Maria, My friend...

My Maria,
My Friend,
My Love.
It's been almost seven or eight years since I was struck down, broke down and compelled to live in a degree of turmoil, uproar and confusion.
There are others who discarded, deserted, abandoned me and left.
But you my stability, my angel.
Stood strong and intensely by me
You never gave up hope or optimism.
Even though I was struggling to hold on to every string of hope and aspiration.
You always reminded me I would find and discover my way through this dark, depressing and gloomy tunnel.
I feel ashamed that I haven't always been able to reciprocate the support and friendship you've given me.

My Maria,
My Friend,
My Love.
There are times when I haven't been present and nearby in the vicinity...
I know it's not always easy to support, and brace yourself.
And for that you do not even need to be forgiven.

I could never give up hope when I have your
wisdom and intellect by my side.
Encouraging me to always lead my life.
You're always considerate and understanding,
And although you do not always understand, I have
your effortless patience.

My Maria,
My Friend,
My Love.
I'm thankful and grateful for your presence, your
strength and calmness you've given me in leading
my life.
I hope we journey together for many years to
come..

8.A year on...

I know it's been a year.
But I want you to know...
I want you to know you are forever present in
every breath and depth of my being
You are eternally my friend ever present love in this
lifetime.
It's my duty to speak of praise for you and I will
forever keep the beauty and wisdom you brought
into my life beaming and gleaming.
I'm glad you knew how I cherished your presence
in my life.
I'm so glad I told you.
You deserved that praise effortlessly.
I was blessed to have you grace my life with your
presence.
You are my genuine love.

I remember your strength, beauty and wisdom
And how it enriched the goodness in my life.
I've packed this baggage up to take with me
wherever this life's journey may take me.
Each day I take a deep breath and I spare you a
thought and remember the lessons you taught me
Then I move forward with your love and friendship
in tow.
Everyday it's starts to become that little bit
effortless.

I know it's been a year.
But I want you to know...
I want you to know you are forever present in
every gulp of air and intensity of my spirit.
You are forever present in this lifetime everlasting.
It's my duty to speak of praise for you and I will
forever keep the beauty and wisdom you brought
into my life shining and glowing
I'm pleased you knew how I treasured your position
in my life.
I'm so thankful that I told you.
You deserved that approval with ease.
I was blessed to have you grace my life with your
presence.
You are my true love.

9.My Strength/ The fire inside of me.

Some days I arise and I feel nothing but weakness
A little voice inside flickers and wavers
Which I can only call willpower.
This is my trace and glimmer of strength.
The fire that burns inside of me.

Some days I arise and I feel nothing but failure
A little voice inside shines unsteadily and trembles
Which I can only call determination.
This is my hint and shimmer of strength.
The fire that blazes inside of me.

Some days I arise and I feel nothing but frailty
A little voice inside sparkles and hesitates
Which I can only call strength of will and mind.
This is my touch and glisten of strength.
The fire that glows inside of me.

Some days I arise and I feel nothing but
powerlessness
A little voice inside flashes and falters
Which I can only call tenacity.
This is my tinge and twinkle of strength .
The fire that endures inside of me.

Some days I arise and I feel nothing but venerability
A little voice inside glimmers and dithers

Which I can only call resolve.
This is my hint and exuberance of strength.
The fire that lingers inside of me.

Some days I arise and I feel nothing but
helplessness
A little voice inside glows and shudders
Which I can only call steadfastness.
This is my dash and gleam of strength.
The fire that sparks inside of me.

Some days I arise and I feel nothing but weakness
A little voice inside flickers and wavers
Which I can only call willpower.
This is my trace and glimmer of strength.
The fire that persists inside of me.

With this strength, faith and resolution I can
achieve anything.

10.My Mother

My mother is the woman I love regardless of any
misconceptions we have about one another.
She is one of the greatest loves of my life.
When she holds me the warmth embraces and
nurtures me.

She teaches me to be stronger no matter what the
challenges I may face.
She is one of the greatest loves of my life
When she holds me her tenderness holds me close
and cultivates me.

She is one of my greatest friends no matter what
trials I face.
She is one of the greatest loves of my life
When she holds me, her kind- heartedness cradles
and fosters me.

She teaches me to be compelling and powerful in
the face of danger.
She is one of the greatest loves of my life
When she holds me her thoughtfulness holds me in
her arms and encourages me.

She gives me the strength and the vigour to walk
through danger.
She is one of the greatest loves of my life
When she holds me her gentleness sustains and

cherishes me.

Mother, you're the greatest love of my life.

11.My Father...

My Father,
You are constantly dedicated and devoted to me
Throughout the sweeping storms and blizzards
You have an appreciative strength and resolve to
stand by my side,
And I am grateful for that.
You have an understanding and consideration to
carry me through the times I cannot face the world
alone.
Father I love you.

Father,
You have the strength of a fighter and you teach me
to never give up.
Even if the finality of the bell is ringing.
Father I love you.

My Father,
What I have is a high regard for your strength,
wisdom, insight and intellect.
You have a knowledge, awareness and deliberation
to carry me through the times I cannot face the
world alone.
Father I love you.

Father,
You have a consistent and coherent commitment to
me.

Your devotion is unswerving.
Your trust, your dependable faith and belief to carry
me through the darkest nights.
Father I love you.

12.I can't believe…

I just heard the news,
That you had passed on,
I feel like I have a flood of tears to release but I
can't bring myself to cry…
Maybe I'm shocked...
Maybe I can't believe you've passed away...
As I never got a chance to say goodbye.

You were one of the most precious things in the
world to me.
You were so kind, caring and gentle and I know I
reciprocated it with love, care and support
whenever I held your hand.
I can't believe I will never hold your hand, embrace
you or kiss your forehead again.
Now your physical presence is absent from me.
Still, I can't believe you are gone.
As writing this is the closest thing I have to saying
goodbye.

I want you to know I will always cherish your
enriched memories of goodness and your kind,
beautiful and delicate soul.
I will hold onto the positivity of your being.
I will never let go even if I can't believe you are
gone.

I just heard the news,

That you had passed on,
I feel like I have a downpour of tears to issue but I
can't bring myself to weep …
Maybe I'm stunned...
Maybe I can't believe you've gone...
As I never got a chance to say farewell.

You were one of the most treasured things on this
Earth to me.
You were so compassionate, sensitive and calm and
I know I reciprocated it with affection, attention
and assistance whenever I held your hand.
I can't believe I will never hold your hand, embrace
you or kiss your forehead again.
Now your instinctiveness is missing from me.
Still, I can't believe you are gone.
As writing this is the closest thing I have to saying
goodbye.

I want you to know I will always value your
deepened memories of decency and your generous,
exquisite and tantalising essence.
I will hold onto your optimistic being.
I will never let go even if I can't believe you are
gone.

13.Confidence.

I may have aged,
I may have matured.
There's something that always holds me back
Something I can't stop paying attention to.
I'll step forward and come clean it's my self-belief
and my confidence.
There are times when I lack confidence, self-
assurance and poise in my writings and in my life.

Now I know that everyone suffers from the lack of
confidence
Due to fear of losing face,
The fear of losing my way, my manner.
The fear of becoming a laughing stock in front of
everyone.
The fear of being judged as less than everyone.

I may have developed,
I may have advanced.
There's something that always holds me back
Something I can't ignore.
I'll step forward and confess it's my confidence.
There are times when I lack confidence and self-
belief in my writings and in my life.

Now I know that everyone endures a lack of
confidence
Due to the fear of suffering defeat,

The fear of losing my way, my respect.
The fear of becoming a figure of fun and a fool in
front of everyone.
The fear of being pronounced less than everyone.

I'm here to say we are created equal as everyone.
Each of us is no more or no less than everyone.
Each and every one of us should just take a deep
breath
Open the door lift our head high and walk on
through
Into any new or given situation.

Remember we are all born equal into this world
And we are no more and no less than everyone.
Everyone has the right to breathe and exhale freely
And to walk on through in this world.
On this note the fear, the panic and the fright
passes and evaporates.
And I'm filled with bravery, confidence, courage
and audacity in every step I take.

14.Goodbye Part Two.

I'm here stuck in the present holding on to the
strings of the past.
These strings are unravelling as I clutch at them.
How do I move on when memories is all I have left
interwoven?
When this goodbye feels so empty?

Why does this not feel like the beginning of a new
Dawn?
Why does this feel like the ending and the final
conclusion?
When this goodbye feels so empty?

I've shed my tears and cast away my fears regarding
you
I hope and pray that dear God and the universe will
take care of your precious and beloved soul.
Yet this goodbye feels so empty.

I keep thinking I will hear your laughter and your
selfless wisdom down the pathway,
But a part of me knows, understands, articulates
and recognises you are gone.
Yet this goodbye feels so empty.

I need to utilise your shrewdness, your intellect and
calmness to keep your candle burning strong and
brightly.

Yet this goodbye feels so empty.

I'm here stuck in the present holding on to the
strings of the past.
These strings are unravelling as I clutch at them.
How do I move on when memories is all I have left
interwoven?
When this goodbye feels so empty?

15.My True Friend.

You are one of my truest friends
And we've been together for nearly fifteen years.
I'm sorry I can't be there in person
Due to circumstances taking hold.
I hope you understand and you are aware
I'm just a phone call away.
You are one of my true loves of this lifetime
And it breaks and fractures my heart to know I
can't be there with you
During this testing and trying time.
I want you know I'm there with you in spirit and
courage
And I'll never give up trying to support you in any
way I can.

You are one of my most genuine friends
And we've been together for almost fifteen years.
I apologise for not being there in person and
I'm dejected due to conditions taking hold.
I hope you comprehend and
Realise I'm just a phone call away.
You are one of my true loves of this lifetime whom
I feel affection for
And it cracks and smashes my heart to know I can't
be there with you
Throughout this complicated and difficult time.
I want you know I'm there with you in character
and determination

And I'll never give up trying to prop you up in any
way I can.

You are one of my most authentic friends
And we've been together for nearly fifteen years.
I'm unhappy and discontented that I can't be there
in person
Due to the situation taking hold.
I hope you will be familiar with that and
Recognize that I'm just a phone call away.
You are one of my true loves of this lifetime whom
I adore
And it shatters and destroys my heart to know I
can't be there with you
During this taxing and convoluted time.
I want you know I'm there with you in Soul and
strength of mind
And I'll never give up trying to sustain you in any
way I can.

16. This is a love that I never knew.

In the beginning I kept and cherished all my
childish and feathered dreams
When the truth is now that this is a love I cannot
comprehend.
This is a love that I never knew.

In the beginning you loving, caring and generous.
I never knew or saw the signs.
Until slowly the illusion lifted and gave way as you
verbally chipped away at my very soul.
And the confused and clouded mists appeared
Now I realise this is a love I never knew.

In the beginning you were affectionate, kind and
considerate.
I never knew or saw the signs.
Until gradually the delusions rose up and gave way
as you physically disfigured my very body.
And the bewildered and misty haze emerged
Now I realise this is a love I never knew.

In the beginning you were devoted, thoughtful and
gentle.
I never knew or saw the signs.
Until steadily the fantasies elevated up and gave way
as you actually bruised and blemished my very body
and soul.
And the disorientated and murky fog became

visible.
Now I realise this is a love I never knew.

In the beginning I kept and cherished all my
childish and feathered dreams
When the truth is now that this is a love I cannot
comprehend.
This is a love that I never knew.

17.My Old Friend...

It was good to see you again my old friend,
As we were thrown together during turbulent times.
I believe we met as fate intended.
And I was shocked and glad to see you
I apologise for cutting our conversation short.
It was good to see you doing well and progressing
through life
And I'm glad we had an opportunity to exchange
our experiences.

It was pleasant to see you again my old friend,
As we were fearful together during chaotic times.
I believe we met as destiny intended.
And I was surprised and pleased to see you
I express regret for condensing our conversation.
It was lovely to see you doing so well and advancing
through life
And I'm thankful that we had an opportunity to
exchange our insight

It was wonderful to see you again my old friend,
As we were unnerved together during turbulent
times.
I accept as true that we met as luck intended.
And I was stunned and relieved to see you
I made an apology for cutting our dialogue so short.
It was delightful to see you doing admirably and
evolving through life

And I'm thrilled we had a chance to exchange our experiences.

18.Pilgrimage

We've been crying oceans, whilst we've been trying
to climb these mountains.
As we look to each other we realise this life has
been tough and strenuous.
As we glance at each other we acknowledge that our
love runs deeper than the pilgrimage of these rivers.
As we stare at each other we realise that our hate
could destroy us and we could be washed away...

We've been weeping in the deep-sea, whilst we've
been trying to rise up these mountains.
As we look to each other we recognise that this life
has been rough and hard- hitting.
As we glance at each other we concede that our
love and affection is full of meaning, stronger and
more robust than the pilgrimage of these waters.
As we stare at each other we realise that our hate
and detestation could damage and ruin us and we
could be swept away...

We've been expressing grief on this ocean floor,
whilst we've been trying to escalate up this foothill.
As we look to each other we comprehend that this
life has been coarse and brutal.
As we glance at each other we concede that our
love and adoration is deep, and more profound than
the pilgrimage of this running stream.
As we stare at each other we realise that our hate

and revulsion could harm and devastate us and we
could be brushed away…

We've been crying oceans, whilst we've been trying
to climb these mountains.
As we look to each other we realise this life has
been tough and strenuous.
As we glance at each other we acknowledge that our
love runs deeper than the pilgrimage of these rivers.
As we stare at each other we realise that our hate
could destroy us and we could be washed away...

As we gaze at each other we grasp and understand
that life's pilgrimage is sturdy and durable as is our
love.
And we cannot and will not allow the hate to tear us
apart and annihilate us.
I admit and accept our love is more powerful,
passionate and potent than that.

19.My Troubled Friend...

I was shocked to hear you took your own life.
I tried to call you many times and I was worried
when I didn't get the response.
Now I know why...
We were together throughout the darkest of nights
and days without daylight.
Throughout our conversations and laughter you
never gave the indication that you wanted to die.
We talked about a subject which I won't mention
here.
Which troubled you as you hurt someone and you
could not forgive yourself for it?
I wish there was something more I could have done
for you, if only you had opened up more.
If only I had read between the lines.
I feel responsible partly as we were close together
for a length of time.
I don't think I could have done more than I already
did.

I was upset and shaken to hear you took your own
life.
I tried to call you many times and I was concerned
and anxious when I didn't get the response.
Now I know why...
We were together throughout the gloomy nights
and depressing days without daylight.
Throughout our discussion and banter you never

gave the indication that you wanted to die.
We talked about a topic which I won't mention
here.
Which distressed you as you hurt someone and you
could not forgive yourself for it?
I wish there was something more I could have done
for you, if only you had opened up more.
If only I had been more receptive.
I feel guilty partly as we were close together for a
length of time.
I don't think I could have done more than I already
did.

20.At the turn of the year.

At the turn of the year,
I reminisced about you, about us and what you
meant to me.
I want you to know you enriched the lives of those
you left behind
With kindness, warmth, love and generosity
And you had such a striking beauty that you are
never forgotten.
I can't thank the universe or nature enough for
allowing you to leave your beauty,
To leave an influence on my life.
I want you to know we are all blessed to have your
beauty imprinted on our lives.

At the turn of the year,
I recalled memories about you, about us and what
you meant to me.
I want you to know you enhanced the lives of those
you left behind
With compassion, affection, friendship and open-
handedness
And you had such an attainable exquisiteness that
you are certainly not forgotten.
I can't thank the creation or the natural world
enough for allowing you to leave your
attractiveness, to leave an influence on my life.
I want you to know we are all blessed to have your
beauty imprinted on our consciousness.

At the turn of the year,
I recollected memories about you, about us and
what you meant to me.
I want you to know you enriched the lives of those
you left behind
With kind-heartedness, tenderness, fondness and
big-heartedness
And you had such a realistic splendour that you are
by no means forgotten.
I can't thank existence or nature enough for
allowing you to leave your magnetism,
to leave an influence on my life.
I want you to know we are all blessed to have your
beauty imprinted on our souls.

21.Angel in the wings.

To you I can express and confide my deepest
darkest fears and secrets.
You are always there on the other end of the phone
listening and waiting patiently.
My Angel in the wings.

I have so much to apologise to you for
My beloved Angel in the wings.
I apologise for not being able to reciprocate our
friendship always as my fears and suspicions have
taken over.
Still there you are in a distance waiting patiently and
tolerantly.
Your support for me does not unravel regardless of
the issues I'm dealing with.
Even though I may unravel my Angel in the wings.

I have so much forgiveness to ask you for
My adored Angel in the wings.
I need to say sorry for not being able to give in
return as always as my uncertainties and
reservations have taken over.
Still there you are in a distance waiting
uncomplainingly and generously.
Your support for me does not come undone
regardless of the issues I'm dealing with.
Even though I may untangle my Angel in the wings.

Yet I have so much to praise you for
My treasured Angel in the wings.
Your many positive attributes,
Your friendship, strength and beauty.
As well as your encouragement and assistance
which never wavers.

As to you I can express and confide my deepest
darkest uncertainties, doubts and worries.
You are always there on the other end of the phone
listening and waiting patiently.
My Angel in the wings.

22.Under the veil of friendship/ The man who I could not love..

I know that you knew secretly I was not yours
But someone else's to damage, ruin and scupper.
That did not stop you pursuing me under the veil of
friendship.
I cared for you no more than a friend.

You knew I cared and was attracted to another
And was fascinated by another
I cared for you no more than a friend.
That did not stop you pursuing me under the veil of
friendship.

I was absolutely spellbound by him.
Even though he was not noble or worthy.
I was attracted to his wit and sense of humour.
I cared for you no more than a friend.
That did not stop you pursuing me under the veil of
friendship.

You sensed I was hurting and wounded by the fact
he did not reciprocate or respond to my feelings.
Although he knew how I felt.
I cared for you no more than a friend.
That did not stop you pursuing me under the veil of
friendship.

You were always there as my dependable, loyal and

trustworthy friend.
You saw my weakness and tried to take advantage
of my pain.
I cared for you no more than a friend.
That did not stop you pursuing me under the veil of
friendship.
I cared for you no more than a friend.

I need to tell you I no longer find you dependable
and trustworthy as my friend.
As you cannot stop pursuing me under the veil of
friendship.

23. Trapped.

I hear your negativity in a distance
I'm trapped within the walls of my mind.
I have no control over the words spoken or over
any images presented.
You interrupt my thoughts in my body in the worst
and most unpleasant ways possible.

I hear your unconstructive and harmful thoughts in
a distance.
I'm trapped within the walls of my mind.
I have some control over some of my thoughts,
But none over any thoughts and images presented
in a distance.
You interrupt my thoughts in my mind in the worst
and most awful ways possible.

I hear your unnecessary and uncooperative
thoughts in a distance.
I'm trapped within the walls of my mind.
I have some control over some of my thoughts,
You interrupt my thoughts consistently in my mind
in the worst and most terrible ways possible.

I hear your needless and pointless thoughts in a
distance.
I'm trapped and crippled within the walls of my
mind
I have some control over some of my thoughts,

You interrupt my thoughts consistently in my mind
in the worst and most terrible ways possible.

24. The Seasons

The end of summer approaches and the autumn
draws closer.
The seasons changing along with me
As I shed my petals and leaves once again
And I let go of a pain so deep-rooted
It evaporates into the Sun.
I learn to live and laugh again.

The end of summer approaches and the autumn
draws closer.
The seasons altering along with me
As I discard my petals and bushes once again
And I release an agony so deep-seated
It disperses into the Sun.
I realise how to be alive and express amusement
again.

The end of summer approaches and the autumn
draws closer.
The seasons shifting along with me
As I get rid of my petals and undergrowth once
again
And I unleash the suffering so embedded
It vanishes into the Sun.
I understand how to survive and giggle again.

The end of summer approaches and the autumn
draws closer.

The seasons transforming along with me
As I cast off my petals and greenery once again
And I let loose of a sorrow so inherent
It dissolves into the Sun.
I ascertain how to breathe and chuckle again.

25.Inspired.

Is there a word for inspiration
Or is it just an idle term?
Does it roll off the heart with such flippancy,
with such an ease,
that it renders one senseless
So inspiration is no longer an idle term
it no longer quantifies the immeasurable

Focused upon your beauty,
the different shades of light and love form a fusion.
So calling this fusion explosive would add to the
illusion forming.

But I do not wish to detract from this fusion.
As your beauty has been unleashed, breaking
through,
radiating to the essence of my being.

Shall I call you an illusion?
Or should I call this perspective
rather than truth

As the truth is so hard to find
even though the heart stirs
even though the heart awakens
there is no certainty
there is no uncertainty

Yet I am shocked into submission
with such ease my soul surrenders
to your will or is that mine?
as my eyes are wide open
absorbing you slowly, as always
You're intoxicating.

If I probe the beauty of your creation any longer
I could slowly collapse and drown within it
I surrender to you completely

Someday I would like to walk across your ocean and
reciprocate the calm you have given me.
As I've unravelled before your eyes so often.

Our fusion is timeless and formless,
we are whole always.
Sometimes I cannot experience that I am still
awakening from my ignorance.
Where does the truth lie in your fusion?
Where does the truth lie in these textured colours?

You're my tapestry, and I am your reflection
Can this be portrayed in any other manner?
After all we are creation, we are creativity.

I am your tapestry, you're my reflection.
Is there any other way to pursue this confusion
down this path?

Or does fate intend for me to carry this confusion
as baggage?

I believe I can break free of this confusion by
releasing it and relieving it.

If you are my reflection it's time to unravel,
It's time to hang onto the string
and release it gently.
At this moment we're no longer...

I have been emptied and rendered senseless.
In stillness and silence alone
Temporarily we are whole.

26.When I write...

When I write I want to write from the heart.
With sensitivity and concern.
When I write I want to say a statement about other
people, myself and the human
condition.
With understanding and kindness.
I want the reader to understand I'm only human
I'm only a person just like them.
Sometimes I get it right sometimes I don't.
All I can say is when I write,
I write from the heart.

When I write I want to write from the spirit and
mind.
With empathy and compassion.
When I write I want to make an assertion about
other people, for myself and the human
circumstance.
With warmth and indifference.
I want the reader to understand I'm only an
individual and I'm only a Soul just like them.
Sometimes I get it right sometimes I don't.
All I can say is when I write,
I write from the heart.

ABOUT THE AUTHOR

It's not so easy giving up when these words flow so straightforward and
effortlessly.
Because it's the expression of my soul, my spirit, and it's my dream....

I will not surrender as long as these words continue to flow
straightforward, directly and effortlessly.

I cannot give it up, even if it sacrifices my time and I pray it will not
prove costly.
Because it's the outpouring of my soul, my spirit, and it's my dream.

Printed in Great Britain
by Amazon

47384154R00036